LEVEL 3 READER

Horses & Ponies

By Sheila Perkins

SCHOLASTIC INC.

Photos ©: cover wood sign and throughout: nevodka/Shutterstock, Inc.; cover ponies: Zuzule/Shutterstock, Inc.; cover horses: Vera Zinkova/Shutterstock, Inc.; cover barn boards and throughout: Bonnie Watton/Shutterstock, Inc.; cover frame: Carl Saathoff/Shutterstock, Inc.; 1 horses: shimmo/iStockphoto; 1 rope and throughout: Сергей Москалюк/Thinkstock; 3 horse: Mike Watson/Thinkstock; 3 frame and throughout: eyewave/Thinkstock; 3 horseshoe and throughout: Ingram Publishing/Thinkstock; 4: Jim Parkin/Thinkstock; 5: Erin Castillo/Thinkstock; 6: Ingram Publishing/Thinkstock; 7 people feeding horse: sonyae/Thinkstock; 7 apples and carrots: dionisvero/Thinkstock; 8: Paige White/Thinkstock; 9 horse: cynoclub/Thinkstock; 9 salt bag: vikif/Thinkstock; 10: muha04/Thinkstock; 11: Rachel Potvin/Thinkstock; 12: Alexia Khruscheva/Thinkstock; 13: Alexia Khruscheva/Thinkstock; 14 Piebald: rosalind morgan/Thinkstock; 14 Appaloosa: vikarus/Thinkstock; 14 Lipizzan: deymos/Thinkstock; 14 Palomino: anakondasp/Thinkstock; 14 Gray: anakondasp/Thinkstock; 15 Stripe: virgonira/Thinkstock; 15 Star: Maria Itina/Thinkstock; 15 Chestnut: Peter Lilja/Media Bakery; 16 left: virgonira/Thinkstock; 16 right: Alan Egginton/Thinkstock; 17: Maria Itina/Thinkstock; 18: Andrew Howe/Thinkstock; 19 left: DragoNika/Shutterstock, Inc.; 19 right: Makarova Viktoria/Shutterstock, Inc.; 20: Meghan Balogh; 21 left: Rohappy/Thinkstock; 21 right: Zuzule/Thinkstock; 22: virgonira/Thinkstock; 23: SuppalakKlabdee/Thinkstock; 24 left: Schlegelfotos/Thinkstock; 24 right: virgonira/Thinkstock; 25 top, 25 bottom: Eric Isselée/Thinkstock; 26: Rick Hyman/Thinkstock; 27 left: Rita Kochmarjova/Shutterstock, Inc.; 27 right: marlenka/Thinkstock; 28: Labrador Photo Video/Shutterstock, Inc.; 29: Tom McGinty/Shutterstock, Inc.; 30 top: meunierd/Shutterstock, Inc.; 30 bottom: CristinaMuraca/Shutterstock, Inc.; 31: gorillaimages/Shutterstock, Inc.

Library of Congress Cataloging in Publication Data available.

Lexile is a registered trademark of MetaMetrics, Inc.

ISBN 978-0-545-88959-9

10 9 8 7 6 5 4 3 2 1   16 17 18 19 20 21

Printed in the U.S.A.   40
First printing, January 2016

Book design by Carla Alpert

Do you know what animal can laugh, wear shoes, sleep standing up, and run almost as soon as it's born?

If you guessed a horse, you are correct!

Humans have been using horses for transportation and work for more than 5,000 years. Today, **domesticated** horses can be found in every part of the world. Mongolia, located between Russia and China, is the only country that still has truly wild horses.

Horses live between 20 and 30 years. A mare, which is a female horse, will carry her foal for about 11 months before giving birth. A foal is a horse that is under one year old. Once it is a few years old, a male foal is called a colt. It will grow to be a stallion. A female foal is called a filly. Once fully grown, it is considered a mare.

A newborn foal grows quickly by drinking its mother's milk, just like a human baby. But one way that foals are very different from babies is that a foal can stand on wobbly legs as soon as it is born. Within a few hours, it can even run!

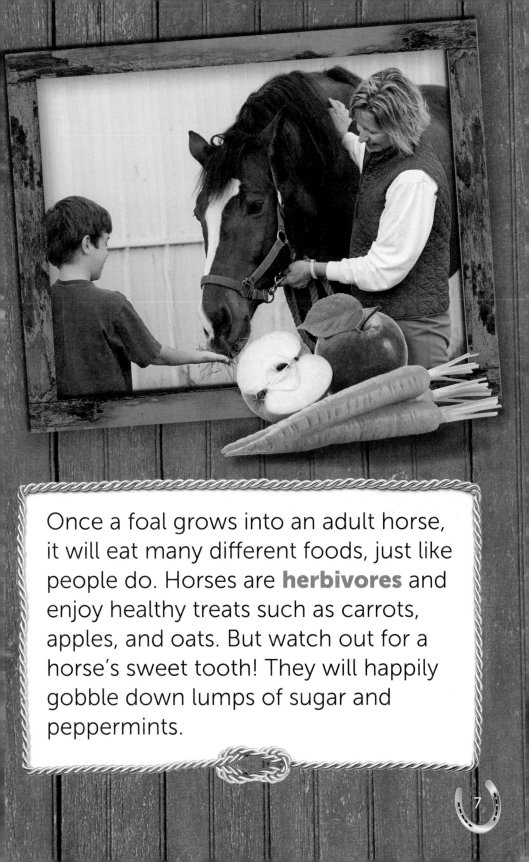

Once a foal grows into an adult horse, it will eat many different foods, just like people do. Horses are **herbivores** and enjoy healthy treats such as carrots, apples, and oats. But watch out for a horse's sweet tooth! They will happily gobble down lumps of sugar and peppermints.

Ponies may look like young horses, but they are very different animals. Even though they are smaller, they are extremely strong. Their manes and tails are thicker than those of horses. Their heads and necks are also stockier, and their legs are shorter. Because of their size, ponies are often more comfortable for children to ride. They are very hardy, which means they can survive in extreme weather and on very little food.

Shetland ponies make great pets because they are good-natured. Another type of pony, the Welsh pony, is considered by many to be a very beautiful breed. They have tiny, pointed ears, large eyes, and wide nostrils.

Ponies can lose a lot of salt when they sweat. You may see them licking salt, which helps them replace the nutrients they have lost from sweating.

Horses and ponies are able to live in a variety of environments, as long as there is plenty of fresh air and water. When they are in a **pasture**, they graze on grass. In the winter, they stay indoors more and eat hay. Rainy days help clean a horse's coat, just like a shower. Their coats grow thicker in the winter to keep them warm, and they like to wear blankets or rugs for extra warmth. A stable keeps a horse warm in cold weather and protects it from the hot sun in the summer.

Horses and ponies sleep on many types of "beds." Straw, sawdust, pine needles, and even newspapers are laid out on the floor of a stall so that horses have a soft place to lie down. But don't be fooled if you see a horse standing perfectly still. They can even sleep standing up!

Body parts on a horse are called **points**, and they are measured by **hands**. A hand is 4 inches. That means that if a horse is 15 hands tall, it is actually 60 inches from its withers (the tallest point between its shoulder blades) to the ground.

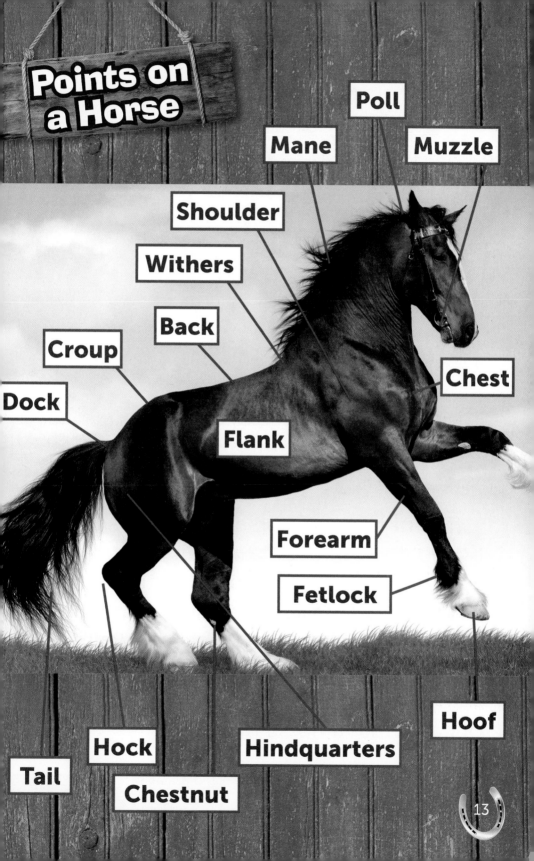

Points on a Horse

Poll

Mane

Muzzle

Shoulder

Withers

Back

Croup

Chest

Dock

Flank

Forearm

Fetlock

Hoof

Hock

Hindquarters

Tail

Chestnut

13

Piebald

Appaloosa

Lipizzan

Palomino

Gray

Different types of horses can be identified by the color of their coats. Lipizzans are born with a black coat that turns white as they grow older. Appaloosas are unmistakable, with black and white spotted coats. There are also gray, dun, palomino, piebald, and many other types of coats that a horse may have.

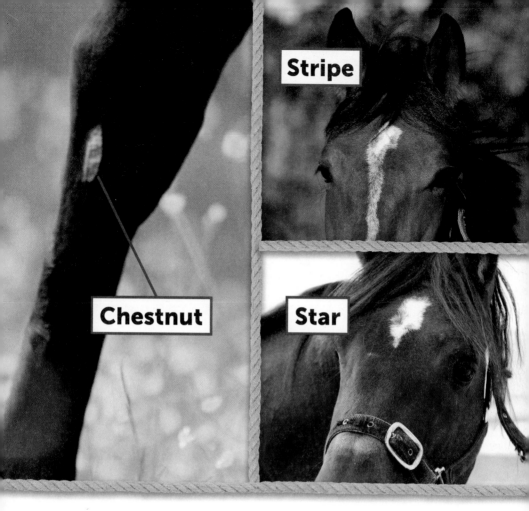

Stripe

Chestnut

Star

Some horses have markings on their faces and legs that look like stars, stripes, or stockings. Their big teeth take up more space in their head than their brain does! But the most unique points on a horse are the four chestnuts. Located on the inside of each leg, a chestnut is to a horse what a fingerprint is to a person.

Did you know that horses have the largest eyes of any land mammal? Their eyes are positioned on the sides of their faces, which means they can see better sideways than in front of them. When a horse grazes with its head down, it can see in a wide arc. Sometimes a horse will wear blinders so that it has to concentrate on what is in front of it. Luckily, horses have sensitive hearing to make up for their poor vision. They can turn their ears in almost any direction and can hear much better than people.

There are more than 200 breeds, or types, of horses. They grow into different shapes and sizes with various colors of coats. The Arabian horse is one of the oldest domesticated breeds in the world. Many believe it is the most beautiful horse of all. It is also one of the strongest and fastest breeds.

Shire horses are tall and strong. They can pull heavy wagons. Shire horses look like they are wearing white socks, but that's really just the long, white hairs that cover their feet.

Falabellas are the smallest horses in the world. They stand only 8 hands tall when fully grown. They may look like ponies, but they are actually miniature horses.

Another breed, Andalusians, are so regal that famous artists such as Leonardo da Vinci have used them in their sculptures and paintings.

The Abaco Spanish Colonial is a special breed and the rarest of all horses. It is descended from the Spanish horses that Christopher Columbus brought to the New World. Unfortunately, there is only one Abaco left in the world, and the breed is in danger of becoming extinct.

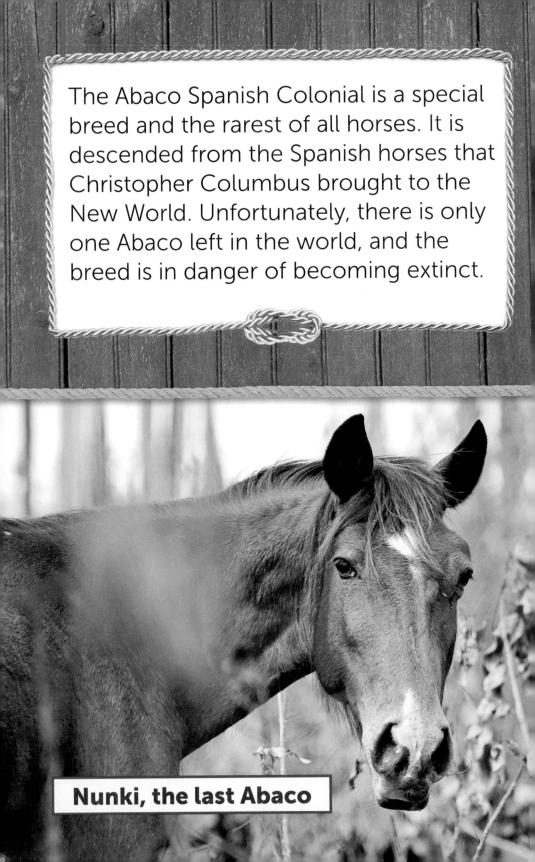

Nunki, the last Abaco

All horses have four different **gaits**, or ways to move. Walking is the slowest gait. Trotting is a little bit faster and looks like a jog. Cantering, or loping, is a faster pace, and galloping is the fastest of all. Most horses can gallop about 30 miles an hour. Quarter horses, which are popular in America, can go as fast as 50 miles an hour. That's as fast as a lion!

Horses are not simple animals. They develop relationships with humans, and they use their bodies and faces to communicate their feelings. If a horse is angry, it will swish its tail back and forth very quickly. If a horse is alert or excited, it will stand tall with its ears perked up. Their moods can change, especially if they sense danger. Some horses are nervous, some are timid, and some are aggressive. They are able to "talk" with people and each other through sounds like snorting, whinnying, and neighing.

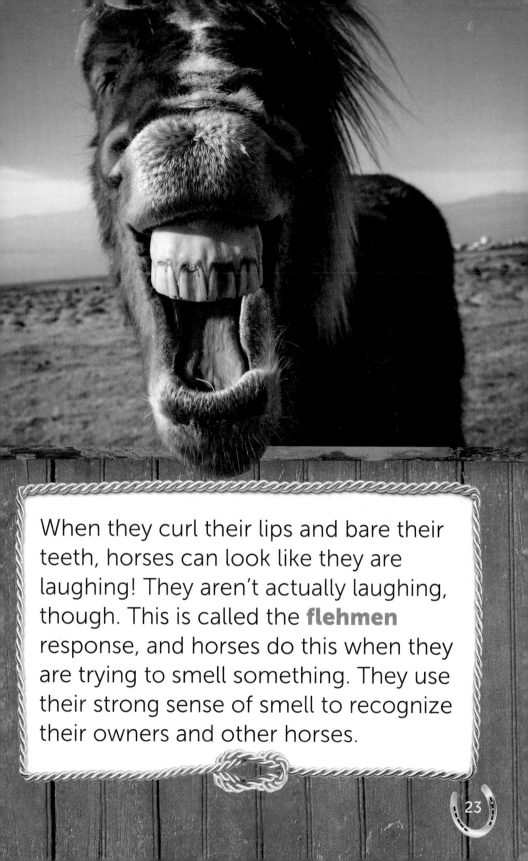

When they curl their lips and bare their teeth, horses can look like they are laughing! They aren't actually laughing, though. This is called the **flehmen** response, and horses do this when they are trying to smell something. They use their strong sense of smell to recognize their owners and other horses.

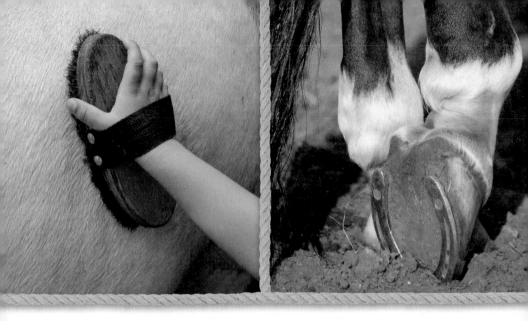

Taking good care of horses and ponies, also known as "handling," requires a lot of work! Stalls need to be "mucked," or cleaned out, regularly. Grooming is important to keep them happy and healthy, and some horses need to have their manes and tails trimmed. Body brushes are used to brush their coats. And don't forget the shoes! Horses and ponies need their hooves protected as they grow. Even after they've been shod, which is when horseshoes have been fitted onto their hooves, they need them to be cleaned every day with a hoof pick.

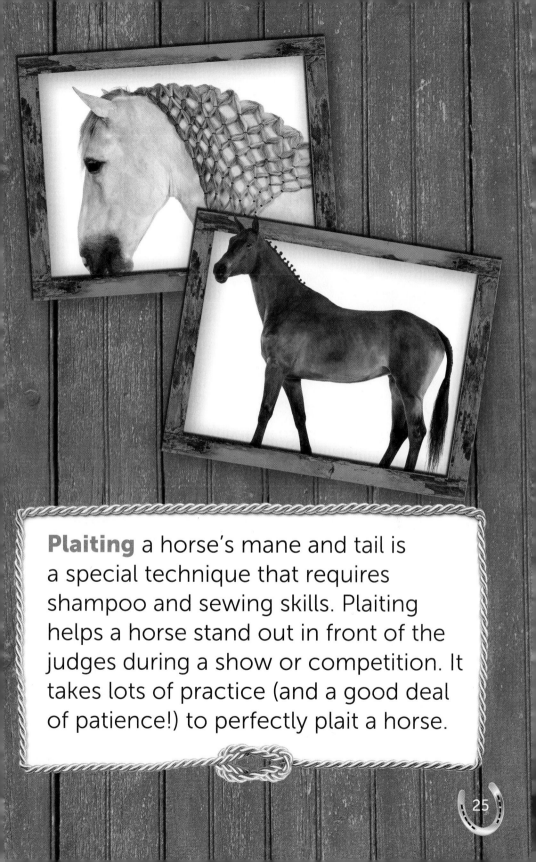

Plaiting a horse's mane and tail is a special technique that requires shampoo and sewing skills. Plaiting helps a horse stand out in front of the judges during a show or competition. It takes lots of practice (and a good deal of patience!) to perfectly plait a horse.

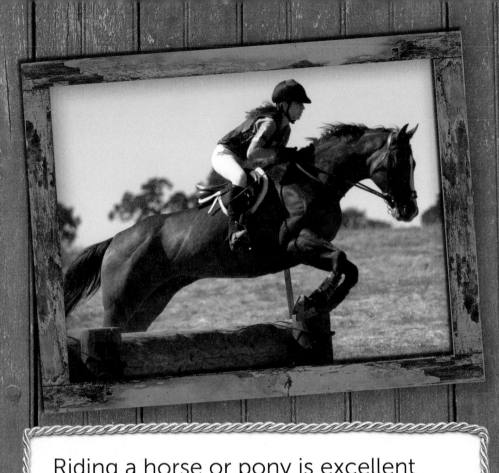

Riding a horse or pony is excellent exercise for both the animal and the rider. Farms and **equestrian** centers provide trail rides and longer courses, which are sometimes called endurance rides. Instructors can teach you how to lead, mount, ride the gaits, and rein a horse. More experienced riders can learn special skills such as pole work and jumping.

Jumping a horse requires a lot of balance and hard work. Some horseback riders compete in shows where they jump their horses through a course of high fences. There are also **dressage** competitions, where the horse and rider train to move together in harmony, almost like dancing! For horse races, the Thoroughbred is the most popular breed because it is very fast, strong, and brave.

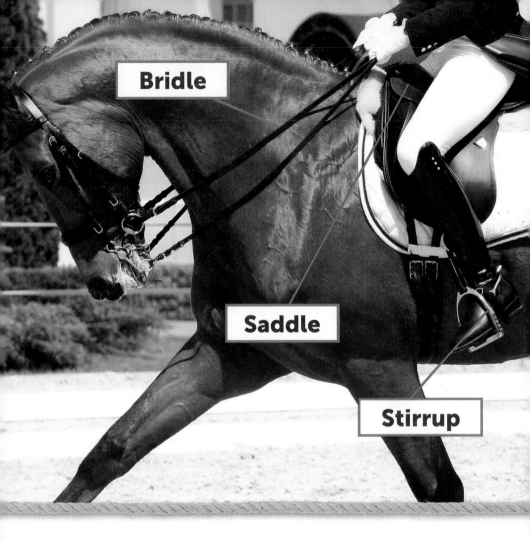

Bridle

Saddle

Stirrup

A horse's **tack** is extremely important for all styles of riding and jumping. The saddle, bridle, and stirrups must be secure and comfortable. At an equestrian center, you can learn how to saddle up a horse or pony and clean the tack after riding.

Horses and ponies can be a lot of fun, especially when you get to compete with your horse in a **gymkhana**! Gymkhanas are games played on horseback within larger competitions. Popular games include the sack race, ball and bucket, and the stepping stone game.

But it's not all fun and games! Horses are used for important work as well. Police officers use them to patrol streets in big cities. Ranchers use them to herd cattle. Large breeds such as the Percheron can pull heavy loads. And before cars were invented, horses and horse-drawn carriages were one of the best ways for people to travel.

People have formed bonds with horses and ponies for thousands of years. All breeds are naturally fearful at first, but they are very smart and compassionate animals. With the proper training and handling, horses and people can develop enough trust to accomplish wonderful things together.

Glossary

Domesticate: to tame a horse or pony so that humans can use them; they are no longer wild

Dressage: training a horse to move precisely with its rider, often as part of a competition

Equestrian: a person who rides horses or ponies

Flehmen: the way a horse or pony curls back its lips in response to a particular smell or taste

Gaits: the four different ways a horse moves: the walk, the trot (sometimes called a jog), the canter (sometimes called the lope), and the gallop

Gymkhanas: fun games played on horseback during larger riding competitions

Hands: the way to measure a horse or pony's height; each hand is 4 inches long

Herbivore: an animal that eats plants and does not eat meat

Pasture: grass, plants, or ground on which a horse or pony can graze or eat

Plaiting: a grooming technique where the mane and tail are washed, brushed, and braided to make a horse or pony look nice, especially before a competition

Points: the parts of a horse or pony's body, such as withers or chestnuts

Tack: all parts of the saddle and bridle; "tacking up" means putting the saddle and bridle on the horse or pony